Highland Railway Album

Title page :   The last Highland Railway engine in
service was the 0 — 4 — 4 tank No 45, built in 1905,
which was still working the Dornoch branch as late
as 1957. In the previous year, she had been
overhauled and would doubtless have worked the
Branch until closure in 1960 had the leading axle
not broken. A GWR pannier tank was used as a
replacement. No 45 is seen here as BR55053
crossing Telford's causeway with the morning train
from Dornoch.   *(W. J. V. Anderson*

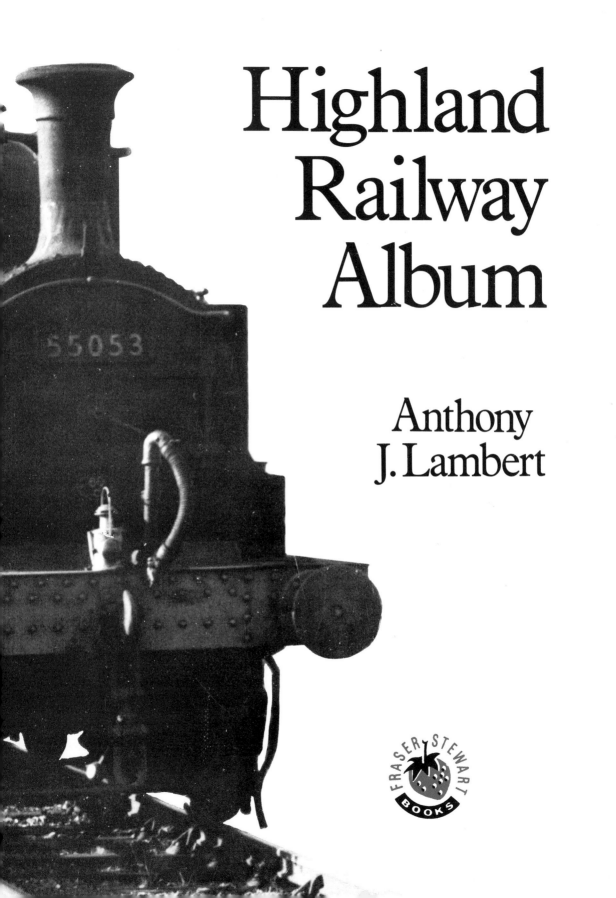

Highland
Railway
Album

Anthony
J. Lambert

FRASER STEWART BOOKS

In memory
of my
Mother and Father.

First published 1974 by Ian Allan Ltd
This edition published 1994
By Fraser Stewart Wholesale Ltd,
Waltham Abbey, Essex.
Produced by the Promotional Reprint Company Limited

ISBN 1-85648-187-5

Printed in India

Introduction

The attraction of the pre-grouping railways, by their very nature, tended to lie in their individuality. Partisans of the various companies often strive to point out such features as may be peculiar to their own company. In the case of the Highland Railway, this is an easy task, for every facet of the railway showed a strong individuality which was largely determined by a combination of the topography, climate, and the social and economic requirements of the railway.

Until the coming of the first railway in 1855 between Inverness and Nairn and the subsequent rapid expansion of the system, the highlands had been a very insular area in which sheep farming and fishing had come to be the main industries since the highland clearances. Travellers venturing north of Perth were relatively uncommon although Telford, Wade and John Mitchell had done much to improve the roads and harbours serving the area. It is probably no exaggeration to say that the railway prevented further depopulation of the highlands by enabling the few staple industries to compete on better terms with those areas nearer the great centres of population. The importance of the railway itself as an employer should not be disregarded, for in an area of low population density any increase in available jobs will naturally be significant. The railway gave rise to the tourist industry which has gone from strength to strength and the stories of the huge entourages of the aristocracy which annually travelled over the Highland Railway to partake of the many sports available, bear witness to the importance of such custom to the railway.

This, and the nature of agricultural transport demands, tended to give a seasonal aspect to the railway's traffic which, although hardly conducive to good business, at least enabled the maintenance staff to undertake repair work that the pressure of the summer months had made impossible. The tremendous increase in traffic occasioned by the war ended this winter hiatus and it became apparent how crucial it had been as the condition of the locomotive stock deteriorated to an unprecedented extent.

To an area in which industrial development is low, the significance of a railway is paradoxically as important in a social context as in a more urban region. The railway will serve to attract some industry and because per capita income is likely to be lower in a predominantly rural area, the populace relies heavily on cheap and reliable public transport. This factor goes a long way to explain why the Highland became an integral part of the lives of all those served by it and probably why the sense of loyalty and esprit de corps developed to such an intensity that traces of it are still perceptible among the older railwaymen, despite the passing of over fifty years since the grouping.

The stories which are told of the days when the railway existed as an independent concern reflect the strong character and individuality of the highlanders. There was a shepherd north of Helmsdale who strung up a few pheasants in some birch trees close to the line and regularly altered their positions. Word soon got around that this was a good place for game and firemen would prepare for it by gathering a pile of suitable lumps of coal which they threw at the decoys, thereby providing the shepherd with a good supply of fuel! Another story concerns a livestock special travelling south from Inverness during the autumn cattle sales. A Jones' Goods was working the train which was nearing the summit at Dalnaspidal when the coupling of the leading van snapped. The driver quickly reversed his engine while the fireman scrambled over the coal and down on to the back of the tender, standing on the buffer and coupling hook and holding on to the horizontal handrail. As the engine caught up with the descending vans, the fireman managed to slip the engine coupling over the leading van's hook and thereby enabled the train to be brought to a stand. The company rewarded his bravery with a cheque for £5, a considerable sum in those days.

Many photographs in this selection testify to the pride of the staff in their job. Such was the regard that the drivers had for their engines that they hardly considered them as belonging to the company, and goods trains were started as gently as passenger trains as a matter of course. The standard of cleanliness expected at stations was exemplary and one inspector of stations was noted for opening a door and running his hand along the top of it. A letter in the author's collection demonstrates that the appearance of the staff was of equal importance: on the 18th December, 1919, the stationmaster at Achterneed was notified by the Traffic Manager's Office in Inverness: "It is reported that your pointsman was wearing a tweed cap when examining tickets on 11am train of 15th inst. Please say as to this".

But these attitudes were typical of the pre-grouping railways and it is to the field of railway engineering that one must look to appreciate the worth and initiative of the Highland. The peculiar operating difficulties fostered an independent approach to problems and this stimulated major advances in railway engineering and locomotive design which remained in the forefront of British practice from the time David Jones took over at Inverness. The story of the introduction of the 4−6−0 wheel arrangement to British railways by Jones has been well documented.[1] The Highland was one of the first railways to experiment with Stone's system of electric lighting in their carriages but they abandoned the idea following problems with battery storage and regular breaking of the dynamo belts.[2]

The railway's worst enemy, snow, required a wide variety of precautions: Point rodding had to be boxed in and signal wires elevated to prevent them from freezing up; the line had to be protected from drifts by erecting snow fences, usually made of old sleepers, and in later years by snow blowers which were designed to use the wind to keep the lines free from snow. Three sizes of snowplough were provided and as soon as snow fell a pilot engine was sent out to clear the line between the running of service trains. In severe winters, three engines were coupled together to perform this duty and such was the weight and pressure of the snow that was thrown up by the large plough that the fence bolts at the lineside often gave way and a pinging sound would accompany the engines' passage. Nor was it unknown for the horizontal steel plates on a footbridge to be lifted right up when engines were clearing snow between platforms. On one occasion, it was necessary to warn passengers at Helmsdale not to lean out of the windows for any distance as the walls of

snow in a cutting gave so little clearance to the train that any protrusion would have caused an accident.

Actual blockages of the line have diminished since the turn of the century as experience of coping with such conditions has been gained by the staff responsible. In more recent times, highland winters have been milder and diesel locomotives have yet to be tested in severe weather.

Today the Highland Railway is still largely intact, the only main section of line now closed being the old route to Inverness from Aviemore to Forres. How long such a state of affairs will continue depends largely upon government policy as both the Kyle and Wick/Thurso lines receive substantial grants. The closure of the Kyle line seems imminent at the time of writing but the future of the further north line, at least as far as Invergordon, seems secure with the great increase in traffic in connection with the British Aluminium smelter there. Closure of either line would be short-sighted for the ever-growing car and human population will render such tourist orientated lines increasingly useful, quite apart from their social importance in linking isolated communities with market towns.

Visitors to the highlands can look forward to the prospect of seeing steam hauled trains once again on a Highland line. The Strathspey Railway Company, assisted by the Strathspey Railway Association, is in the process of re-opening the section from Aviemore to Boat of Garten. A considerable collection of locomotives and rolling stock has been assembled which will be kept in the large Highland engine shed at Aviemore. Among the engines are LMSR Black Five No 5025, already magnificently restored, LMSR 2−6−0s 46512 and 46464, and Wemyss Private Railway 0−6−0 tank engine No 17. It is hoped that the privately owned Caledonian Railway 0−6−0 No 828 will be removed from its present home in the Scottish Museum of Transport in Glasgow and transferred to Aviemore for work on the line. With such a popular holiday area to draw upon, the success of the venture seems assured.

1 Brian Reed, *Jones Goods & Indian L,* Profile Publication 1971.

2 Readers interested in rolling stock are recommended to D.L.G. Hunter's *Carriages & Wagons of the Highland Railway.* Turntable Enterprises 1971.

Right: The poster which marked the inception of railways in the Highlands. Andrew Dougall remained secretary and general manager at Inverness for forty-one years until his retirement in 1896. *(J. Cook*

OPENING
OF THE
INVERNESS & NAIRN RAILWAY.

THE Public are respectfully informed that MONDAY, 5th November 1855, being fixed for the OPENING DAY, the Directors have resolved upon giving the Inhabitants of IN-VERNESS an opportunity of enjoying a

GRAND PLEASURE
EXCURSION TRIP
TO NAIRN & BACK.

On that day the Trains will run at the following Hours, and the Fares reduced as under:—

Leave INVERNESS at 12 noon.
Returning from NAIRN at 3 p.m.

FARES: Going and Returning--
Covered Carriages, 2s. ; Open do., 1s.

On TUESDAY a similar advantage will be given to the In-habitants of NAIRN, and on WEDNESDAY, following day, the Line will be Opened for Public Traffic; and for the Hours of the Trains, Fares, &c., see other bills.   By Order.

AND. DOUGALL, General Manager.

INVERNESS & NAIRN RAILWAY COMPANY'S OFFICE,
Inverness, 31st October 1855.

[Printed at the Advertiser Office.

Top left: Glenbarry class No 31 *Princess* of 1863 in original form before rebuilding as a 2 − 4 − 0 by David Jones in 1884. Such features as the two safety valves on a domeless boiler, 'Allan type' chimney and lift-up smokebox door remind one how rapidly locomotive design on the HR advanced between the Glenbarrys of 1863-4 and the 4 − 4 − 0 Duke class of 1874. *(Locomotive Publishing Co*

Centre left: Of the eighteen Glenbarry singles, No 32 was the only engine not converted into a 2 − 4 − 0 and remained a single until withdrawn in 1898. No 32 was first named *Sutherland* but for some reason exchanged names with No 55 *Cluny* when the latter was rebuilt in 1874. *Cluny* is seen here outside the shed at Dingwall with Jones chimney and new smokebox. *(Real Photographs*

Bottom left: Inverness and Aberdeen Junction Railway No 11 was the last of a class of seven locomotives, built in 1858/9, which were the first engines designed specifically for working goods

trains on the railway. It was a sister engine, No 10 which had the distinction of becoming the Highland's first 4 − 4 − 0 when it was rebuilt in 1873 as a precursor of the 'Skye Bogies'. *(R. J. Essery Collection*

Above: in 1862, two 2 − 4 − 0s, Nos 14 and 15 were supplied by Hawthorns for goods work on the Inverness and Ross-shire section. They were later fitted with larger driving wheels and cylinders by Jones and No 14, given the number 6 in 1893, is seen in this form. *(A. G. Ellis Collection*

Below: William Stroudley standing on the footplate of I & AJR 18 class No 21, built in 1863. Before leaving for Brighton, Stroudley introduced three varieties of snow-plough to cope with varying depths of snow. The type on No 21 was the largest, designed to tackle ten foot drifts and of wooden construction. *(J. Cook*

Top left: Although No 2 *Aldourie* has been classified as a rebuild of the Inverness and Nairn Railway single of that name, the engine which emerged from Lochgorm in 1871 amounted to a new locomotive with new boiler, frames and cylinders. *Aldourie* survived until 1903 and is seen here outside Lochgorm works. *(A. J. Bowie*

Centre left: Following the policy of designing 2−4−0s for goods traffic and singles for passenger, Barclay enlarged the 18 class to produce the 36 class of which ten were built, all in 1864. Jones rebuilt both classes in their entirety. Here No 38 stands outside the roundhouse at Inverness in unrebuilt form. *(Locomotive Publishing Co*

Below left: David Jones succeeded Stroudley as locomotive superintendent in 1870 and constructed the last two new 2−4−0s for the HR in 1877 at Lochgorm. *Raigmore* and *Ballindaloch* ran until 1912 and 1910 respectively. *(Locomotive Publishing Co*

Above: The contrast between the primitive Glenbarry single and the same engine after conversion to a 2−4−0 by Jones is remarkable. No 46 was rebuilt in 1880 and in 1883 the original name of *Clachnacuddin* was transferred to Duke class No 71 which was built in that year. No 46 was renamed *Kingussie* and is seen here at Perth. *(Locomotive Publishing Co*

Below: Photographs of 2−4−0s working trains are rare. Here an unidentified rebuild leaves Forres with a train for Keith. The signal-box is Forres East, the only one of three Forres cabins still in operation. *(A. G. Ellis Collection*

Above: No 7 began life in 1858 as a 2 – 4 – 0 goods engine on the I & AJR but following the opening of the line to Strome Ferry in 1870 it was soon found that the rigid leading axle on the 2 – 4 – 0s did not suit the sharp curves. Accordingly, Jones rebuilt sister engine No 10 as a 4 – 4 – 0 in 1873 and No 7 was similarly converted in 1875. These engines were the predecessors of the 'Skye Bogies'.
(Locomotive Publishing Co

Below: It was not until 1882, nine years after the conversion of No 10 that Jones combined the boiler, cylinders and motion of the Duke class 4 – 4 – 0s and the small driving wheels of Nos 7 and 10 to produce the well-known 'Skye Bogies'. Even then there remained a single example of the class until 1892. No 85 is seen here at Kyle in 1906.
(L & GRP

Top right: No 88 was completed at Lochgorm in 1895. Although used predominantly on the Kyle line, these engines were employed north of Dingwall and No 88 is seen here standing outside the shed at Helmsdale.   *(G. Seaton*

Centre right: David Jones became locomotive superintendent in 1870 but it was not until 1874 that his first design appeared with the Duke or F class 4 – 4 – 0 which set the pattern for new locomotives until the 'Big Goods' of 1894. No 69, originally *The Lord Provost,* was the last of the 1874 batch of ten engines built by Dubs.   *(A. J. Bowie*

Bottom right: Duke No 62 had three names before receiving in 1903 the name *Ault Wharrie* which was the residence of J. G. Stewart, Dunblane, a director of the railway. When these engines appeared in 1874, they were the largest and heaviest locomotives in Great Britain.
(A. J. Bowie

Above: No 65 *Nairnshire* at Inverness shed. The 1874 series was built with these outside-framed 1800 gallon tenders on which the communication cord to the gong may be clearly seen. An unusual feature is the jack mounted behind the coal. When carried, this was normally on the running plate. *(Locomotive Publishing Co*

Right: This photograph of No 79 *Atholl* standing by the Loco Box at Inverness exemplifies the interest then taken in the appearance of locomotives. Even the bogie frame is lined out. The occasion for which the engine was decorated is not

recorded but the two crowns would suggest a Royal Train. The Jones characteristic of transversely-mounted safety valves may be seen to advantage. *(Inverness Museum*

Below: No 89 *Sir George* was the first of the twelve Straths which were built in 1892 by Neilson & Co. Basically similar to the Duke 4 — 4 — 0s, the Straths had larger boilers necessitating a shorter chimney which together made them look more solid if less elegant.   *(Mitchell Library*

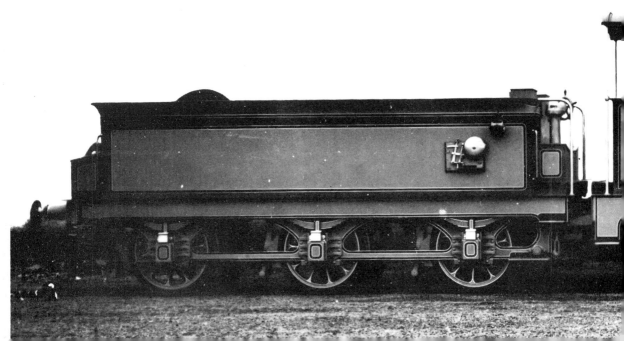

Above: 82 *Durn* was one of the final series of eight Duke class engines, all built in 1886 by the Clyde Locomotive Co. They were similar to the earlier two batches save a shorter boiler and longer firebox The boiler pressure was also higher. No 82 is seen here at Blair Atholl with one of Drummond's 0 – 6 – 4 tanks on the right. *(Photomatic Ltd*

Below: A local train on the Highland headed by Strath No 100 *Glenbruar.* The location is unknown but this engine was frequently on the Kyle line and at Achnalt, the signal wires were carried on posts. The running of fitted goods vehicles in passenger trains was normal procedure on the Highland and such vehicles, luggage vans, meat vans, fish trucks etc. were accordingly painted in passenger colours. *(Locomotive Publishing Co*

Above: In later years, a regular duty of the Straths was piloting trains to Druimuachdar Summit and here a Strath and a Castle are seen leaving Blair Atholl with a northbound express.
(H. C Casserley Collection

Below: The fifteen Jones 'Big Goods', all of which were delivered in 1894, were the first 4 – 6 – 0s to be built for a railway in Great Britain. It has been suggested that the occasion is the commencement of No 113's first run over the Highland main line, the photograph being taken at Stanley Junction, but this is a matter of conjecture.
(A. G. Ellis Collection

Top left: No 108 in workshops grey with the large type of snowplough used to clear 10 or 12ft drifts. Three of the class, Nos 106 – 108, had supports fitted to the side of the smokebox to enable them to carry the large snowploughs. A special bracket on the chimney was provided for the top lamp. *(Real Photographs*

Centre left: No 112 on the turntable at Inverness with sister engine No 107 in the background. Both these engines lost their smokebox wing plates at an early date for no apparent reason.

Bottom left: As may be seen in this photograph, the 'Big Goods' were built with flangeless drivers but there was a tendency for them to drop off the rail and thin flanges were fitted to most engines. No 116, seen here at Perth, was one of two Jones

Goods fitted with Westinghouse brake apparatus to cope with through coaches from the Caledonian and East Coast Joint Stock constituent companies. *(Locomotive Publishing Co*

Above: No 110 amidst typical scenery on the main line near Dalwhinnie. During the 1914-18 war the 'Jellicoe Specials' were, on occasions, hauled by two 'Big Goods' over this line. *(L & GRP*

Below: The 4 – 4 – 0 Loch class was Jones' last design and these engines were amongst the most powerful in the country when new. Fifteen of the class were built in 1896 and a further three in 1917 when the HR was under great stress and desperately short of engines. No 124 was photographed when new at what is thought to be Stanley Junction. *(A. G. Ellis Collection*

Top left: Photographs seldom do justice to Jones's lavish lining as the red and black are usually indistinguishable, leaving an impression of only white to relieve the black bands. This photograph of No 129 *Loch Maree* at Perth is perhaps a case in point. *(Locomotive Publishing Co*

Centre left: No 119 *Loch Insh* in the evening sun at Perth shed. This engine carried the Prince of Wales's feathers on the leading splasher after hauling a special train conveying the Duke of York, later King George V, from Perth to Grantown in September 1896. *(Locomotive Publishing Co*

Below left: After the grouping, Caledonian boilers were fitted to the class which ruined their appearance as wing plates seemed to suit Highland

engines particularly well. Old No 131 *Loch Shin* is shown standing outside Perth shed in its rebuilt form in LMS days. *(Locomotive Publishing Co*

Above: The Strathpeffer Spa Express was the only regular train to run through Inverness without stopping and was designed to promote the growing spa where the railway company had opened a hotel on 1st June, 1911. The train began from Aviemore, connecting with a Perth train, and was usually hauled by a Loch. No 129 *Loch Maree* is seen here on the duty. *(Real Photographs*

Below: The negative for this photograph of a Loch and Clan hard at work was amongst a batch quite recently rescued from sale as glass. It is unusual in showing the sanders of the leading engine in operation. The Loch is No 123 *Loch An Dorb* in LMS livery. *(G. W. Osborne*

Top left: No 1 *Ben-y-Gloe* at Perth probably soon after delivery from Dubs & Co as the 'Small Bens' usually worked north and east of Inverness. Designed by Peter Drummond, the first of these engines appeared in 1898 and the last in 1906. *(BR*

Centre left: No 10 *Ben Slioch* by the side of Lochgorm Works. Nine of the twenty 'Small Bens' were built at Lochgorm, making them the last tender locomotives to be constructed at the company's workshops. Although these engines became popular with the enginemen, there were reservations at first partly because they were the first tender engines with inside cylinders on the Highland. *(Locomotive Publishing Co*

Bottom left: This delightful photograph of No 2 *Ben Alder* on the turntable at Inverness roundhouse conveys the sense of pride the driver had for his regular engine. When an engine went into the workshops, the driver often accompanied it to make sure everything was done to his satisfaction. *(Locomotive Publishing Co*

Above: No 14 *Ben Dearg* against the familiar rock backcloth at Kyle of Lochalsh shed. No 14 was one of four 'Small Bens' fitted with an eight-wheel tender. Under Frederick Smith, the numberplates were replaced by painted numerals higher up on the cab side and aluminium numbers on the smokebox were added. *(Locomotive Publishing Co*

Below: The Royal Train hauled by No 10 *Ben Slioch* at Welsh's Bridge Junction on the 8th September, 1902. King Edward VII and Queen Alexandra had disembarked from the Royal Yacht and were journeying to Ballater. *(A. J. Bowie*

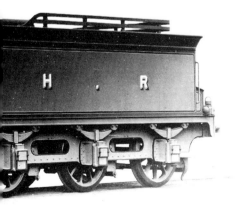

Top left: It is a matter of debate whether Drummond's 0—6—0s were ever referred to as 'Barneys' by the drivers but a poem published by a stationmaster during the First World War to raise funds for the Red Cross mentioned 'Barneys'. Drummond goods or 'Barney' No 138 with medium snowplough is seen here piloting No 74 *Durn* at Wick in March 1924.   *(K. A. C. R. Nunn*

Above: Apart from the Callender and Oban line, Highland engines rarely ventured far from their home territory after the grouping and when they did it was seldom for passenger work but No 17703, HR No 36, is seen here on such duty at Glasgow Central in 1938.   *(H. C. Casserley*

Left: Drummond's 'Barney' 0—6—0 goods engines first appeared in 1900, having the same boiler and cylinders as the 'Small Bens'. No 18 was a batch of four built in 1902 with water tube fireboxes and six-wheel tenders.   *(Mitchell Library*

Top left: No 134 in immaculate condition, probably taken soon after delivery in 1900 as four of the first batch of six engines soon lost their double-bogie tenders to 'Small Bens'.
(Locomotive Publishing Co

Centre left: No 19 poses for what was probably an official HR photograph. The abundance of lining on what was only a goods engine serves to remind one how prosaic our railways have become.
(Author's Collection

Left: The Castle class was a natural development for passenger work of the 'Big Goods' with larger boiler and driving wheels. The first of the class No 140 *Taymouth Castle* was completed in 1900. Inheriting the basic design from Jones, Drummond made only minor modifications before placing an order for six engines with Dubs.
Mitchell Library

Above: No 144 *Blair Castle* immaculately groomed and decorated for the 'Further North Grand Press Tour' which was a series of specials run in early June 1906 for London journalists.
Inverness Museum

Top left: A Perth to Inverness train which has travelled via Forres waits to leave Nairn behind No 141 *Ballindaloch Castle.* These engines proved so successful that the class eventually numbered nineteen by 1917. The water-tower on the right is of unconventional construction and might date back to I&N days. It was demolished by 1913. *(Locomotive Publishing Co.*

Centre left: This posed photograph of No 144 *Blair Castle* with artificial backcloth was produced for publicity purposes. The HR was well aware of the importance of promotional advertising and at one time had a decorated road van touring Great Britain to publicise the attractions of the highlands. *(BR*

Bottom left: In 1908 the Western Railway of France was taken over by the State and shortly after, a serious shortage of motive power occurred. To overcome the problem with a minimum of delay, an order was placed with the North British Loco Co for fifty locomotives to the design of Drummond's Castle. No 230-338 is seen here leaving Poissy in 1912. *(Kelland Collection*

Above: No 145 *Murthly Castle* on a stopping train south of Dalwhinnie. Note the heavily strengthened telegraph poles to withstand the ferocity of highland storms. *(Inverness Museum*

Below: No 230-328 in use in France. Apart from minor modifications such as taller chimney, re-arranged rear splasher, solid coal rails and fatter dome casing, they were identical to the Highland engines. *(La Vie du Rail*

Above: Photographs of the 1917 batch of three Castles in HR livery are uncommon. Certain modifications were made including an increase of 3in in the coupled wheels to give 6ft, minor firebox alterations and a six wheel tender of enlarged capacity. No 50 *Brodie Castle* is seen here waiting at Perth to work a train to Inverness. *(Bucknall Collection*

Below: No 145 *Murthly Castle* pilots No 51 *Clan Fraser,* in LMS livery, on a train consisting of Midland, North British and Highland coaches and a Pullman car. *(G. W. Osborne*

Top right: The six 'Big Bens', built in 1908/9, were basically similar to the 'Small Bens' but had a larger boiler with higher pressure. The last two engines, one of them No 60 *Ben Bhreac Mhor,* were built with double-bogie tenders of 3,600 gallons capacity. *(L&GRP*

Centre right: No 66 *Ben Mholach* at Perth when new. The engine only carried this number for a year being renumbered 64 in 1909. The first four 'Big Bens' were built with six-wheel tenders of 3,185 gallons as seen here but two of them were later given double-bogie tenders off 'Barney' 0-6-0s. Greater coal capacity must have been the reason for this exchange as the increase in water capacity was a mere fifteen gallons! *(Locomotive Publishing Co*

Bottom right: *Ben Mholach,* now No 64, at Blair Atholl with a northbound train. Although the motion and cylinders were identical to that on the 'Small Bens', it is surprising to note that the tractive effort was the same, as their larger boilers gave them a sturdy and more capable appearance *(A. G. Ellis Collection*

Top left: After F. G. Smith's resignation over the River class, Christopher Cumming became locomotive superintendent and his first design was a superheated 4—4—0 for the mail trains on the Wick line. No 73 *Snaigow* and No 74 *Durn* were the first 4—4—0s built in the UK with outside cylinders and Walschaert valve gear for a British railway. *(Locomotive Publishing Co*

Centre left: No 73 *Snaigow* at Wick with a small wooden snowplough. The two engines were built by Hawthorn, Leslie & Co and entered service in 1917. The crest mounted below the name on the splasher became a feature under Cumming. *(K. A. C. R. Nunn*

Bottom left: The first four of Cumming's design of goods engine appeared in 1917, No 75 being the first, the final four not being delivered until 1919

by which time traffic was returning to normal proportions after the war. Behind No 75 is one of the four London and South Western Railway's Adams 4—4—2 radial tanks which were loaned to the HR during the war. Photographs of any of the forty-two engines which were on loan are naturally rare. *(Real Photographs*

Above: No 78 inside the shed at Perth. The last of these powerful engines could still be seen at work on the Kyle line as late as 1952. *(K. A. C. R. Nunn*

Below: These engines were not confined to goods workings as this photograph of No 77 climbing to Druimuachdar Summit shows. Their versatility even extended to the working of ten coach trains over the Perth line. *(L & GRP*

Top left: The last engines built for the Highland Railway were eight passenger locomotives designed by Cumming and named after Highland clans. The first four appeared in 1919 and the remainder in 1921. No 55 *Clan Mackinnon* is seen here at Perth. *(Real Photographs*

Centre left: No 55 *Clan Mackinnon* near Strathord on the Caledonian line between Stanley Junction and Perth. The adornment of the engine's smokebox by the regular driver was a common practice which still persists in some continental countries. *(L & GRP*

Bottom left: Two Clans at Aviemore. It is thought to be the south end in which case No 55 *Clan Mackinnon* will have brought the Inverness train and No 49 *Clan Campbell* will have travelled via Forres. The title of 'Clan goods' for Cumming's earlier 4—6—0 arose as a result of the similarity between them and these larger engines. *(R. M. Campbell*

Above: Although of rather indifferent quality, this photograph has been included since it shows the experimental Scarab oil burning system fitted to No 53 *Clan Stewart* in 1921. Although successful, the experiment was not developed probably due to the grouping. *(R. Berry*

Below: The Findhorn Railway began life as an independent concern but in 1862, after two years of operation, financial difficulties arose and the I & AJR took over the working of the three mile branch from Kinloss to Findhorn. This 1859 Neilson 0—4—0 which had worked the branch was also taken over and became No 16 before being sold to a firm of contractors in Wick who used it while constructing the Sutherland and Caithness Railway. *(R. J. Essery Collection*

Top left : No 59 *Highlander* was one of three
2—4—0 tanks built at Lochgorm in 1878/9.
Trouble was experienced with the rigid leading
axle and the three engines were converted to
4—4—0 tanks in 1881/2.   *(BR*

Centre left : This diminutive tank was built by
Hawthorns in 1863 as an 0—4—0 for the Burghead
line which it worked until 1879, but it proved
unstable so Stroudley added a trailing bogie. After
performing minor duties at Forres and Inverness,
the number of 17 was removed, a cab fitted and
the engine named *Needlefield.* It is in this state in
the photograph. After working as a stationary
engine in Lochgorm Works and futher minor
alterations, the engine was sold in
1902.   *(Author's Collection*

Bottom left : No 57 *Lochgorm* was built by Jones in
1872 to a design by Stroudley who later developed

it into the well-known Terrier tank engine on the
London, Brighton and South Coast Rly. Stroudley
had built the first of this design, No 56 *Balnain,* in
1869 and Jones added a further example in 1874.
Balnain was the first engine to be built at
Lochgorm Works.   *(A. G. Ellis Collection*

Above : The rebuilt No 58 *Burghead,* probably
photographed at that fishing port as No 58,
worked on the branch from its rebuilding until
1892 when two new Yankee tanks were sent to the
line.   *(Locomotive Publishing Co*

Below : This ungainly-looking single tank was
originally 2—2—2 No 12 *Belladrum* until
converted in 1871 for use on the Aberfeldy branch
In 1885, the engine was reboilered and the name
changed from *Breadalbane* to *Strathpeffer* on
which branch the engine was put to work before
withdrawal in 1898.   *(A. G. Ellis Collection*

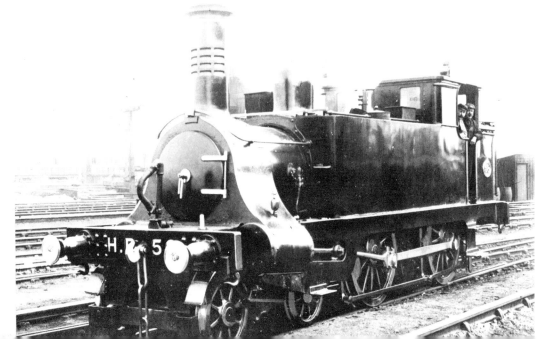

Top left: Three 0−6−0 tank engines were built at Lochgorm in 1903/4 from parts taken from withdrawn 2−4−0 goods and passenger engines. This gave rise to the knickname of 'scrap' tank. They were intended for shunting work but No 24 did operate on the Fortrose branch for a time. No 23 is seen here at Inverness.
(Locomotive Publishing Co

Centre left: By 1890, the old single tank engine which had been built by Jones in 1871 needed replacement and Jones accordingly built this 0−4−4 tank with inside cylinders which were then unusual on the HR. The boiler was not new, having been taken off 2−2−2 No 13 and shortened.   *(Real Photographs*

Bottom left: No 58 at Inverness after losing its name in 1900. The tank held 700 gallons but No 17

was fitted with an 850 gallon tank for working over the Aberfeldy branch.   *(Real Photographs*

Above: In 1901 *Strathpeffer* was rebuilt at Lochgorm with a new boiler and side tanks and two years later was renamed *Lybster* in readiness for the opening of the branch to that fishing village. *Lybster* was the regular engine for many years and is seen here as LMS No 15050 at Wick shed.   *(H. C. Casserley*

Below: This attractive 0−4−4 tank was built by Drummond at Lochgorm in 1905 to work the branch serving the spa after which it was named. Three other engines of the class were built and they were the last engines to be constructed at Lochgorm Works.   *(A. J. Bowie*

Left: In 1891 the Uruguay Eastern Railway refused delivery of two tank engines from Dubs & Co and the HR bought them after a year's trial. The American trappings were removed but the slide-bar covers were initially retained.
(Mitchell Library

Top left: The Highland must have found the two trial engines very satisfactory for they ordered three more which were delivered in 1893. No 14 one of the first two was sent to relieve No 59 *Highlander* on the Portessie branch.
(H. C. Casserley Collection

Above: No 102, one of the three additional engines, was rebuilt by Drummond in 1906, with a larger boiler and extended coal bunker, and was later named *Munlochy.* The engine is seen here at Fortrose in 1913.   *(L & GRP*

Left: Drummond's last design for the Highland Rly before he left for Kilmarnock was an $0-6-4$ tank which was intended primarily for use on banking duties. Eight were built over three years, the first, No 39, appearing in 1909. It was unusual for the tablet-exchange apparatus to be fitted by the makers, this task normally being left until the arrival of the new engine at Inverness.
(Mitchell Library

Top left: These handsome engines were the largest tank design for the Highland and weighed 69½ tons. Three of the class were renumbered to provide consecutive numbers for the 'Big Bens'; No 66, which is seen here at Dalnaspidal after banking a train, being originally No 64.   *(L & GRP*

Above: As this photograph of No 44 shows, these engines were not confined to banking duties but worked goods trains and even passenger trains. It may be noticed that these engines retained the Highland peculiarity of a lamp bracket on the right-hand side of the tender, in this case above the numberplate on the bunker.   *(Locomotive Publishing Co*

Previous page: The 'River' class being banned for weight and clearance reasons was a tragedy for the Highland not only because they had to sell six excellent engines but also because it was later found that the methods of stress calculation for bridges were unnecessarily severe which enabled the Rivers to return to the Highland section in 1927. This photograph shows a River and Big Ben restarting a southbound train out of Killiecrankie. *(J. H. L. Adams*

Below: Perth engine shed c1904. From left to right, Castle No 143 *Gordon Castle* inside the shed, No 130 *Loch Fannich,* 'Barney' 0 − 6 − 0 No 18 inside the shed and another of the same class, No 139 and Duke 4 − 4 − 0 No 83 Monkland. Towards the end of the 1914-18 war the stone gable at the north end, seen here, was replaced by a wooden structure. *(H. C. Casserley Collection*

Above: The HR had running powers over the Caledonian Railway from Stanley Junction to Perth, the southern extremity of the Highland system. Here a local train, probably from Blair Atholl, is seen passing the ticket platform at Perth behind 4 − 4 − 0 No 91 *Strathspey.* *(L & GRP*

Top right: Ballinluig station, junction for Aberfeldy, seen from across the River Tummel. The branch train may be seen in the platform. *(Author's Collection*

Centre right: A northbound train, headed by a Castle, on Killiecrankie viaduct which cost a mere £11 5s per lineal foot. The vegetation has so re-established itself that it is no longer easy to photograph satisfactorily. *(A. J. Bowie*

Bottom right: Killiecrankie station looking south. Note the signal wires carried on posts to prevent being rendered inoperable in snow. *(H. C. Casserley Collection*

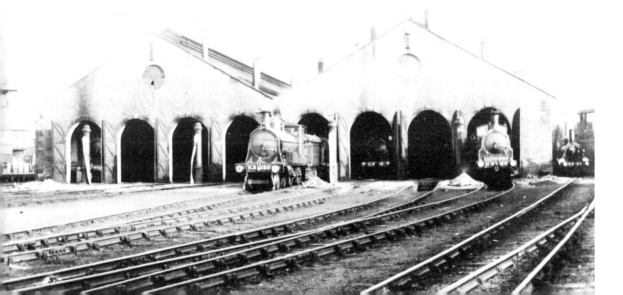

Above: Struan station looking south in 1915. The station buildings date from 1898 when they were built to replace an earlier structure burnt down in October 1897.   *(Perth Museum*

Below: Blair Atholl station looking south. One wing of the station building has been demolished recently which has ruined the symmetry of the attractive structure.

Above: An 0 — 6 — 4 tank (LMS No 15307 formerly HR No 44) at Dalnaspidal, the highest station served by a main line in the British Isles, where the bankers to Druimuachdar summit crossed over to return to Blair Atholl. *(H. C. Casserley*

Below: The engine shed at Kingussie, opened in 1889/90 to accommodate the engines which assisted southbound trains up to Druimuachdar summit. With the introduction of more powerful engines, the need for pilots was reduced and the few remaining workings were transferred to Aviemore shed in 1920.

Above: The old station building at Kingussie. The replacement structure was built behind the old which was then demolished, thereby giving a wider platform. *(BR*

Below: The new station at Kingussie, designed by William Roberts who later became chief engineer, was completed in 1895. Following usual Highland practice, the interior was finished in pitch pine, partly stained and entirely varnished.

(Author's Collection

Above: Grandtully station in 1904 looking towards Ballinluig Junction. The stone cottage in the background is an example of the standard dwelling-house built by the company for its employees, in this case probably the station-master. Note the horse and cart in the goods yard. *(Perth Museum*

Below: An early view of Aberfeldy taken before the original engine-shed was burnt down in 1902. Note the primitive banner signal on the right. Soon after the branch was opened in 1865, proposals were made to extend the line to join the Callander and Oban Railway west of Killin but these came to nothing. *(G. W. Wilson*

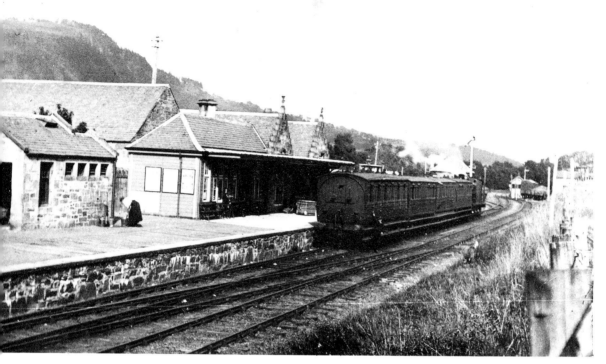

Above: Aberfeldy station looking towards Ballinluig. The engine is one of Drummond's 0 – 6 – 4 tanks, probably No 39 which was on the branch around 1912 when the photograph was taken. The site of the station is now covered by a housing estate. *(L & GRP*

Below: The station square at Inverness on the occasion of the unveiling of the Cameron Statue by Lochiel in 1893. On the left are the company's offices and on the right the station hotel, also owned by the railway. *(J. Cook*

Above: Inverness station in 1906 with No 145 *Murthly Castle* at platform 2. Great North of Scotland coaching stock may be seen at the platforms on which the photographer is standing. *(L & GRP*

Below: The station concourse adjacent to the site of the present booking office. Judging by the advertisement for 'All the war pictures' on the extreme right, it was taken between 1914-18 although it could conceivably refer to the Boer War. *(BR*

Above: The station hotel at Inverness when the main entrance was in Academy Street.
(*G. W. Wilson*

Below: The harbour branch, opened at the same time as the Inverness and Nairn, ran parallel with the line to Dingwall from Rose Street Junction cabin but at a lower level as the main line climbed to cross the River Ness. Here, two horses prepare to take a loaded wagon up to Rose Street cabin. The signal cabin is Ness Viaduct where the double-line ended before the railway crossed the viaduct.
(*Inverness Museum*

Above: The view of Lochgorm Works from the direction of Welsh's Bridge. The lines to the left of the works terminate in the station while those to the right lead to Rose Street Junction for the north and Kyle. On the right is the carriage shed and sidings. Note the East Coast Joint Stock carriages in the centre. *(A. J. Bowie*

Below: The quay where the half-mile harbour branch terminated. The photograph was taken from Ness Viaduct. *(J. Cook*

Top left: An early view of the roundhouse at Inverness. No 12 *Belladrum* built in 1862 to work the Inverness and Ross-shire Railway, was rebuilt in 1871 as a 2—2—2 side tank and named *Breadalbane* (*A. J. Bowie*

Above: One of the machine shops at Lochgorm Works. The machines were arranged in four rows, one down each side of two walls and two back to back down the centre. The tramway continued into the Erecting Shop. (*A. J. Bowie*

Centre left: A later view of the roundhouse. Two of the 0—6—0T locomotives can be seen, which had been constructed by Drummond from scrapped engine parts. (*L & GRP*

Bottom left: The erecting shop at Lochgorm Works. On the left is a boring machine and behind that a slotting machine. On the right is a planing machine. The engines appear to be largely outside-framed which would suggest that the photograph was taken before the turn of the century. (*A. J. Bowie*

Below: An Inverness train headed by a 'Small Ben' at Nairn in 1913. These engines hauled most of the eastbound trains to Keith and from 1906 they worked right through to Aberdeen over GNSR metals. (*L & GRP*

Top left: Forres station with the Keith line platforms on the left and those for Aviemore on the right. After the opening of the direct line to Inverness, the importance of the route via Forres naturally diminished but the line over Dava moor between Forres and Aviemore was not closed until October 1965. *(A. G. Ellis Collection*

Centre left: The south junction at Forres in 1913 taken from the road bridge under which the now closed main line to Aviemore passed. No 96 *Glentilt* may well be waiting to pilot or bank a train up to Dava summit. Factories now surround the station and even the road bridge on which the photographer was standing has now disappeared. *(L & GRP*

Bottom left: The original Spey viaduct, near Orton, which was opened as part of the section between Elgin and Keith in August 1856, thereby completing the rail link between London and Inverness. The commemorative plaques are preserved at Inverness station.
(Central Library, Edinburgh

Right: In 1905/6 the box girder bridge was replaced by one of lattice girder construction using the original abutments. During reconstruction a temporary signal-box with home and distant signals each way was provided at the bridge.
(A. J. Bowie

Below: Orton station in 1937. Between 1858 and 1866, Orton was a junction with the Morayshire Railway which ran to Dandaleith near Craigellachie. Following the construction of their own line between Elgin and Rothes, the GNSR closed the section between Orton and Rothes although the permanent way was not removed until 1907. *(L & GRP*

Top left: In LMS days, two 'Small Bens' 14402 *Ben Armin* and 14408 *Ben Hope* leave Keith with a train for Inverness. Keith East signal cabin, the only cantilever box except Ness Viaduct, may be seen on the right. The Highland shed is on the left. *(A. G. Ellis Collection*

Centre left: Keith, the eastern extremity of the HR, where an end-on junction was made with the Great North of Scotland Rly. The date is 1913 and the photographer is looking east. Note the tiny signal arm under the eave of the station roof. *(L&GRP*

Bottom left: The railway reached Burghead before the amalgamation which created the HR in 1865. The branch opened in December 1862 and left the Keith line at Alves, terminating at a station on Burghead pier. It was the busiest of the Highland branches and a two-road shed was provided at Burghead. It is seen here in LMS days with 3F tank No 16415 outside. *(W. A. Camwell*

Above: The station staff at Hopeman. The extension to this fishing village was opened on 10th October, 1892 when a new station was opened at Burghead at which Hopeman trains could call. Thereafter the old station at Burghead was closed to passenger traffic but the railway continued to serve the harbour. *(D. Mackay*

Below: The branch train waiting to leave Hopeman for Alves behind LMS 3F 'Jinty' tank No 16415 in 1928. *(H. C. Casserley*

Above: The swing bridge and cabin at Clachnaharry. The bridge was originally swung by hand but it is now power operated and takes twice as long to swing. In 1909 the bridge was strengthened and the timber viaduct at Beauly replaced leaving only the Oykell viaduct to prevent anything larger than a 4 — 4 — 0 working to Wick. Beyond the footbridge is Clachnaharry station which closed in May, 1913. *(Author's Collection*

Below: The gauntleted track at Clachnaharry where the doubling of the line to Lentran began in 1901. A conventional turnout was put in beyond the bridge in 1924. Other examples of this interlacing could be found at Norwood Fork Junction and Selby where the lines across the swing bridge were gauntleted. *(Author's Collection*

Above: Muir of Ord station, junction for Fortrose, with 'Barney' No 21 entering from the north in 1913. The heterogeneous composition of the train was typical of the Highland. Note the leading coach which has a coupé end compartment; these were always locked when next to the engine. The station buildings on both up and down platforms were burnt down in November 1922.   *(L&GRP*

Below: Dingwall station on the occasion of the conferring of the Freedom of the Burgh of Dingwall on Lord Rosebery who succeeded Gladstone as Prime Minister in 1894. This ceremony was performed on 10th September, 1894 when Lord Rosebery was travelling south from Dunrobin. The train, an ordinary service train, was delayed for half an hour. On the left may be seen the original refreshment rooms.   *(A. Macrae Collection*

Above: The Strathpeffer mail coach waiting at
Dingwall station, presumably before the opening
of the branch to the spa in 1885. Note the original
station buildings.   *(A. Macrae Collection*

Below: A northbound train of nineteen vehicles
waits to leave Dingwall behind a 'Small Ben' and a
Jones 4 — 4 — 0. The first vehicle with only one pair
of doors is a parcels van while the second is parcel
van No 3.   *(A. J. Bowie*

Above: Culrain station with No 120 *Loch Ness* entering on a southbound train. The standard lattice footbridges on the HR were made at the Rose Street Foundry, Inverness. *(G. E. Langmuir Collection*

Below: The only major bridge north of Dingwall is the Oykell viaduct which crosses the Kyle of Sutherland by a 230ft lattice girder span. It was this bridge that prevented the working of Castles to Wick until strengthening of the ironwork in 1912/13. The single platform of Invershin station may be seen on the north bank. *(P. Beal*

Top left: The Mound, junction for Dornoch, looking north. The date of construction, 1877, may be seen on the station chimney breast. The trackwork is typical — ash ballast up to the bottom of the rail making the sleepers barely discernible — rather like that on the Great Eastern.
(A. J. Bowie

Centre left: A southbound train standing at Invershin station which was one of the few stations on the Wick line without a passing loop. The two carriages and passenger brake van were built in 1873 for the Wick line. An unusual feature of these coaches was the hinging of the door on the right jamb instead of the left as in normal practice.
(G. W. Wilson

Bottom left: Helmsdale station looking out to sea showing the old engine-shed which was blown down in a gale on 15th February, 1921. The engine is probably No 76 *Bruce* which was the Helmsdale

pilot engine for a number of years prior to the grouping. *(Author's Collection*

Above: Georgemas Junction looking south in 1912 with the Thurso branch to the right. Note the flat-bottom rail in the Thurso arrival bay. The Yankee tank taking water is No 54 and would have been the Thurso engine for the Georgemas locals and shunting. One other engine was kept at Thurso shed for the through trains to Wick. The Inverness train engine is a Loch. *(L & GRP*

Below: Wick station on 1st July, 1903 when the Lybster branch was opened. Despite relaying with chaired track in the early war years, the branch was closed completely in 1944. The driver of the first train was present on the closing day. *(Inverness Museum*

Top left: The 8.40am train to Inverness waits to leave Wick with emigrants for Canada in 1912 when a number of local quarries closed. As there was no alternative employment, large numbers emigrated. *(W. Dunnett*

Above: Trains crossing at Achnashellach in 1927. The train entering from Kyle is headed by Skye Bogie No 14283, HR No 33. *(H. C. Casserley*

Bottom left: Although of poor quality, this photograph has been included because it is the only picture of Fodderty Junction known to the author. The Strathpeffer branch is to the left and the main line to Kyle curves off to the right. *(Author's Collection*

Below: The old terminus at Strome Ferry which was burnt down together with fourteen carriages and luggage vans on 16th October, 1891. When the line first opened from Dingwall in 1870, steamers sailed daily to Portree and thrice weekly to Stornoway. *(G. W. Wilson*

Above: Strome Ferry station looking down Loch Carron towards Kyle taken before the line was extended to Kyle of Lochalsh. When the line from Dingwall to Strome Ferry was opened to passengers on August 19th, 1870 the Franco-Prussian War was being fought on the continent and the *Illustrated London News* expected that many tourists would take advantage of the new scenic railway because the continent was closed to them!
(G. W. Wilson

Below: The cutting on the approach to Kyle of Lochalsh. Because cuttings of this nature abound on the last miles, the cost per mile of the Strome Ferry to Kyle section was five times as great as the rest of the Dingwall and Skye Railway. Note the telegraph pole constructed of rail. *(A. Macrae Collection*

Top right: The throat of Kyle station looking towards Skye. When the circular point rodding as seen in this picture was replaced by channel rods it was found to be eminently suitable for wireless aerials and consequently HR point rodding came to adorn many Inverness roofs. *(P. Beal*

Centre right: The station buildings at Kyle looking across the water to Kyleakin. Judging by the freshness of the works, evidence of construction work and absence of passengers and staff, the photograph was probably taken before the opening from Strome Ferry on 2nd November, 1897. Note the outside framed, dumb-buffered wagons on the right. *(P. Beal*

Bottom right: The Portree and Stornoway steamers at Kyle pier looking across unusually tranquil water to the mountains of Skye. The Stornoway steamer in the foreground is the *Lovedale,* built in 1867 and originally owned by the Great Western Rly. The Portree vessel is the *Gael,* also built in 1867 and formerly owned by the GWR, which survived until 1924. *(P. Beal*

Top left: The line from Keith to the sea at Portessie met the GNSR coast line from Elgin to Portsoy. This view of Portessie looking east shows the GNSR on the left and the HR on the right with the Highland signal-cabin marking the site of the platform.   *(L & GRP*

Above: Rathven station looking towards Keith before the signals were removed in May 1907. In the thirty-one years from the opening of the line in 1884 to its closure in 1915, Rathven had only one stationmaster, Allan Kennedy. The slate roof on the signal-cabin was uncommon, corrugated iron being more usual.   *(A. Kennedy*

Centre left: The engine shed at Portessie, the only Highland shed constructed in brick. Dating from the opening of the line in 1884, the shed was closed in March 1909 but continued in existence as a concrete block factory.   *(E. W. Hannan*

Bottom left: Buckie station in 1912. This was probably considered the most important station on the branch as the building had a gable at each end in contrast to the single gable of other stations. *(L & GRP*

Below: In August 1915, services were withdrawn and the track lifted between Aultmore distillery and Buckie and it was not until after the grouping that the line was re-laid. The Highland Railway board was petitioned by Aultmore and other villages to re-open the line but they replied that they were unable to do so because of the shortage of staff. The re-laying in 1923 was accompanied by changing the name of Drybridge station to Letterfourie but services were never resumed. Drybridge station is seen here after re-naming. *(L & GRP*

Top left: The Strathpeffer branch train with No 13 *Strathpeffer*. The 2½ mile branch, opened on 3rd June, 1885 left the Kyle line at Fodderty Junction. The Spa was to have been served by the main line but opposition by a local landowner necessitated the re-routing of the line past Raven's Rock. *(E. McKenna Collection*

Centre left: The Strathpeffer station staff with the branch train. Built at Lochgorm Works in 1890, No 13 was renumbered in 1899 and rebuilt as a side tank in 1901 so the date would be between 1890 and 1899. *(Author's Collection*

Bottom left: A later view of the terminus. No 13 has been rebuilt and dispatched north to work the Lybster branch and one of Drummond's 0−4−4 tanks, No 25 *Strathpeffer* built at Lochgorm in 1905, now works the branch. The date is 1913. *(L & GRP*

Above: Culloden Moor Viaduct during construction on 20th June, 1895, looking east. The line of the contractor's railway from Leanach Quarry may be discerned to the left of the photograph beyond the road. Straddling Strathnairn, the viaduct was 600 yards long with twenty-nine arches. With four major viaducts and the excavation of two million cubic yards of rock and soil, the Aviemore Direct line cost nearly one million pounds. *(N. T. Sinclair*

Below: Culloden Moor station in 1897/8 before the line was opened. The activity at the south end suggests that the connection to the goods yard may be being installed. It was at the station master's house here that Murdoch Paterson, the chief engineer, died on 9th August, 1898 at the age of 72. He had taken up residence in the house to be nearer Culloden Moor Viaduct which was threatening to delay opening of the line. *(N. T.Sinclair*

Above: The party at Carr Bridge on the opening of the line. The photograph is dated 1898 so it was presumably the 1st November when the final section from Daviot to Inverness was opened, to give through running between Aviemore and Inverness. Carr Bridge itself had been opened six years previously.   *(J. Cook*

Below: On 8th July, 1892, a temporary service was inaugurated with the opening of the line from Aviemore Junction to Carr Bridge. This photograph shows one of these trains on Dulnain Viaduct near Carr Bridge. The engine is No 58 *Burghead* which had presumably been displaced from the Burghead branch by the arrival of Yankee Tanks Nos 101 and 102.

(A. G. Ellis Collection

Above: The direct line to Inverness made Aviemore an important junction involving a complete reconstruction of the facilities. This view, looking north, shows work at an advanced stage although neither the signals nor the trackwork leading to the engine shed on the right are complete. Two typical features may be noted: the carrying of signal wires on posts to avoid seizing up in freezing snow at ground level and provision of two water columns for double-headed trains. *(BR*

Below: Aviemore engine shed with a pair of Loch 4—4—0s, 122 *Loch Moy* and 128 *Loch Luichart*, outside. Probably taken soon after the shed was opened in 1898 in conjunction with the direct line. *(J. E. Kite Collection*

Top left: Fortrose station looking towards the junction at Muir of Ord in 1913. 'Small Ben' No 4 *Ben More* has just been turned. This branch of 13½ miles was opened in 1874 and served the fertile promontory of the Black Isle. Passenger services were withdrawn in 1951 and a housing estate now covers the site of the station.
(L & GRP

Centre left: A 'Small Ben' at Fortrose in LMS days with the engine shed and water tower to the right. The branch saw quite a variety of locomotives with 'Small Bens', 'Barneys', Yankee tanks, Scrap tanks and the older Duke class taking turns on branch workings.   *(W. A. Camwell*

Bottom left: The Fortrose train at the branch platform at Muir of Ord. The station building is the replacement structure for the one burnt down in November 1922.   *(H. C. Casserley*

Above: The 1½ mile branch to Fort George was opened in 1899 and built primarily to serve the military establishment although the line actually terminated in the village of Ardersier. This photograph of No 29 *Forres* at the terminus must have been taken soon after the opening, as the engine was withdrawn in 1905.

Below: A later view of the station with Drummond 0 – 4 – 4 tank No 46 working the train. This photograph was taken from a coloured postcard.
(D. Johnstone

Above: One of Smith's River class enters Gollanfield Junction where the Fort George branch left the main line to Keith. The branch train is headed by *Ben Alder,* formerly No 2.

(H. C. Casserley

Below: Fochabers Town station with No 40 *Gordon Lennox* on the branch train. Before the line was opened in 1893, both Spey Bay on the GNSR and Orbliston Junction stations had been named Fochabers although the distance from the town to both was 4 miles. (A. G. Ellis Collection

Above: The only intermediate stop on the line was Balnacoul where Robert Matthew was stationmaster for many years after losing a leg during shunting. *(M. Matthew*

Below: The Fochabers branch train arriving at Orbliston Junction behind 14274, formerly No 95, *Strathcarron* in 1930, the year the engine was withdrawn. A Midland brake supplements the single Highland carriage. Today the bay platform is barely discernible amongst the saplings and undergrowth. *(H. C. Casserley*

Above: The opening of the Dornoch branch on June 2nd, 1902 with local dignataries and directors of the Dornoch Light Railway Company. This concern retained its independence until the grouping although the line was always worked by the HR. Thomas Wilson, then general manager of the Highland, described the occasion as a "red-letter day in the history of the empire!" *(A. J. Bowie*

Below: The station at Dornoch soon after the opening. For a short time the town enjoyed an excellent train service: in 1905 a Pullman car was worked direct to Dornoch on the 12.50am down train and in the following year the 'Further North Express' was inaugurated at the beginning of the summer season. It ran non-stop to The Mound and terminated at Dornoch but this evidently proved unsuccessful as in the autumn the destination was altered to Wick. *(A. J. Bowie*

Above: The engine shed at Dornoch with No 56 outside. The first engine to be built at Lochgorm Works, it was the prototype of Stroudley's Terriers. In 1896 Jones rebuilt the engine and the name was changed from *Balnain* to *Dornoch* for the opening of the line in 1902. *(A. J. Bowie*

Below: The Dornoch train at the branch platform at The Mound, junction with the main line to Wick. The coaches still retain their white upper panels which reverted to green in 1903 so the photograph was probably taken soon after the opening. *(A. G. Ellis Collection*

Above: The junction at The Mound c1902 judging by the lack of vegetation on the embankment. The main line to Wick and Thurso is on the left.
(A. J. Bowie

Below: Lybster station, terminus of the 13¾ mile Wick and Lybster Light Railway which was the last part of the Highland system to be opened although a start was made on a line to Cromarty. The flags and the contractor's engine on the left would suggest that the photograph was taken just before the opening of the line in July 1903. *(A. J. Bowie*

Above: The inaugural train arriving at Lybster on 1st July, 1903 with the director's saloon No 59 as the third vehicle. During the last war it was proposed to extend the branch to Dunbeath for the battle training ground but the War Office rejected the idea and the branch was completely closed in April 1944, although not before the line was relaid with chaired track.   *(A. J. Bowie*

Next page: The party present at the opening ceremony of the line at Lybster station. The Treasury contributed over a third of the subscribed capital and the HR worked the line at cost price. *(Author's Collection*

Below: The engine shed at Lybster shortly after completion with No 53 which was rebuilt from the saddle tank *Strathpeffer* and renamed *Lybster* for the opening of the line.   *(A. J. Bowie*

Top left: The branch train with No 53. The leading carriage is third No 99 built in 1878. *(A. J. Bowie*

Centre left: Fort Augustus Pier station on Loch Ness, probably taken before the line was opened as the works appear to be new and the station was closed in September 1906 when trains terminated at the town station. The Highland worked the line from its opening in July 1903 until the North British took over the working on 1st May, 1907. *(R. J. Essery Collection*

Bottom left: Gairlochy station in 1914 in which year the NBR purchased the Invergarry and Fort Augustus Railway. The history of the line was unusually turbulent being an object of contest between the North British and the Highland. *(R. J. Essery Collection*

Above: An officers' special at Invergarry. The occasion is unknown but may have been an inspection of the line prior to the visit of King Edward VII in 1905. The engine is Skye Bogie No 48. *(P. Beal*

Below: King Edward VII (on the right) at Spean Bridge on the occasion of his visit to Glenquoich in 1905. *(Inverness Museum*

Top left: The Royal Train conveying King Edward VII to Glenquoich skirting Loch Oich near Invergarry station. No 48 was the last of the Skye Bogies, being completed under Drummond in 1901. *(D. Mackay*

Far left: The south end of the crossing loop at Tomatin. The majority of signals on the Highland were supplied by McKenzie and Holland of Worcester as were the examples shown in the photograph. The skeleton-armed signal on the right controlled the entrance to the goods yard

although these arms were also used on wrong-line signals. The typical Highland feature of encasing the point rodding may be discerned on the left beyond the bracket signal. *(Author's Collection*

Centre left: The up home signal of Nairn West cabin and the up distant of Nairn East. This arrangement was typical at Highland crossing points because the loop was almost invariably longer than the stipulated maximum distance over which a facing point could be worked from a signal-box and two cabins, as they were known on the Highland, were consequently necessary. The windlass for winding the lamps may be seen beneath the elegant finial. *(Author's Collection*

Left: A McKenzie and Holland revolving ground signal photographed at Pitlochry in 1970. *(A. J. Lambert*

Above: Dalraddy signal cabin situated between Aviemore and Kincraig shortly after the crossing was taken out of use for the winter in September 1937. Crossing loops to divide lengthy sections between stations were a feature of the Highland and with the reduced traffic of the winter months it was usual to disconnect the points and signals of most of these loops at the end of the summer season. *(A. G. Ellis Collection*

Above: Inchlea, a crossing point between Dalwhinnie and Newtonmore, was the only Highland cabin with an inside staircase. In common with most cabins before 1914, the construction is of timber with rib-sides and corrugated iron roof. This was a particularly unpleasant post in winter as the south loop points were operated by a separate frame and the signalmen's cottages were a long walk from the cabin. *(Dr. I. Scrimgeour*

Opposite: The Manson system of tablet exchange apparatus was adopted by the HR after the mechanism had proved its worth on the Fraserburgh and other sections of the Great North of Scotland Railway. Its working is demonstrated by Strath No 89 *Sir George*. *(Author's Collection*

Below: The alternative to mechanical apparatus may be seen here as the crew of either No 73 *Snaigow* or No 74 *Durn* exchange the tablet with the signalman at Clachnaharry. *(Author's Collection*

Above: Testing the setting of the exchange apparatus at Ness Viaduct, Inverness. The cabin was taken out of use on 18th February, 1934 when the point at the beginning of the viaduct became motor-operated from Rose Street. *(Author's Collection*

Below: Three engines charging a drift of 7ft above rail level on 8th March, 1895 south of Altnabraec. A relatively primitive camera shutter has helped to produce this evocative photograph of what must have been a most impressive sight and sound. *(P. Beal*

Top right: Digging three engines out of a drift near County March between Altnabraec and Forsinard in February 1895. The leading engine is Barclay 2 − 4 − 0 No 43. Note the man on the telegraph pole who will have attached a phonophore to the line. The ability to connect phonophores with the telegraph wires at the scene of trouble and thereby communicate with control via the adjacent stations must have made such winter operations considerably more expeditious. *(P. Beal*

Centre right: One of the many gangs of men which struggled to keep the line clear in the appalling conditions of a highland winter. Taken at Dalnaspidal in 1904. *(Author's Collection*

Bottom right: Barney 0 − 6 − 0 after a battle with the snow. Highland water columns were prevented from freezing by heating the air within the column which enclosed a water pipe of considerably smaller diameter. *(P. Beal*

Top left: The Aberfeldy branch train at the terminus in 1912. The vehicle on the immediate left is 4-wheel passenger brake van No 9 of which type fourteen were built. The next vehicle is first class carriage No 36. The 'pot lamps', as the roof lamps were known, may be clearly seen and a photograph of one appears on a later page. *(L & GRP*

Centre left: One of the two composites built at Inverness in 1898, Nos 47 and 48. Short side corridors connected the four third and three first compartments to two centre lavatories. *(A. J. Bowie*

Bottom left: Drummond had fifteen of these 35ft 8in long luggage vans built at Needlefield, the carriage and wagon works in Inverness, between 1900 and 1903. *(A. J. Bowie*

Above: The first of eight thirds built between 1909 and 1912 following a decision to provide vestibule connections on main line trains to Perth. *(HMRS*

Below: Two of these all third saloon vehicles were built by R. Y. Pickering and Co in 1906 for excursion traffic and were fitted with both vacuum and Westinghouse brakes. Seating fifty passengers, the two saloons were connected by a short corridor which gave access to a lavatory. The external finish was highly varnished teak, an experiment of very short duration but these two coaches and two similarly-treated sleeping carriages built at the same time were not painted in the usual green until the 1914-18 war. *(A. G. Ellis Collection*

Top left: Ten of these 13 ton brake vans were supplied by Pickering in 1898.   (HMRS

Above: In 1914, fifty of these 12 ton coal wagons with end doors were built by R. Y. Pickering and a further fifty followed in the ensuing year.

Centre left: This ingenious device for moving lengths of rail was known as a 'dip-lorry'. The fish wagon was one built in the early 1900s to replace some of three hundred fish wagons built in 1873-4. (*Author's Collection*

Bottom left: One of twenty meat vans built by R. Y. Pickering in 1911. These vans were painted in passenger colours as were all fitted vehicles.

(*A. G. Ellis Collection*

Below: When the first *Dunrobin* was replaced by an 0 – 4 – 4 tank engine in 1895, it was purchased by the Highland Rly for £300 and rebuilt in the form seen here. It was sent to work the Fochabers branch and later renamed *Invergordon* when it was used for shunting at the harbour there. (*Photomatic Ltd*

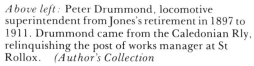

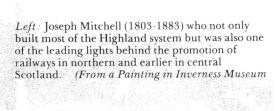

Above left: Peter Drummond, locomotive superintendent from Jones's retirement in 1897 to 1911. Drummond came from the Caledonian Rly, relinquishing the post of works manager at St Rollox. *(Author's Collection*

Above: David Jones, the figure who dominates the locomotive history of the HR. He joined the Inverness and Nairn Railway in 1855 after serving his apprenticeship at the London and North Western Railway Longsight works in Manchester. It was not long after his appointment as locomotive superintendent in 1870 that the Highland took a leading role in locomotive development in Great Britain.
(Author's Collection

Left: Joseph Mitchell (1803-1883) who not only built most of the Highland system but was also one of the leading lights behind the promotion of railways in northern and earlier in central Scotland. *(From a Painting in Inverness Museum*

Above: Alexander Newlands (1870-1938), engineer to the HR from 1914 to 1922. Before this appointment, he was resident engineer on the Dingwall and Skye extension to Kyle and assistant engineer under William Roberts from 1902. *(Inverness Museum*

Above right: The third Duke of Sutherland (1828-1892) who made a singularly generous contribution to railway development in the highlands, particularly that north of Inverness. Until 1948, the Dukes of Sutherland were able to run their own rolling stock over the Highland, and later that section of the LMS. *(From a painting in Dunrobin Castle by courtesy of the Countess of Sutherland*

Right: Cluny Macpherson, Chairman of the Inverness and Nairn Railway from its inception in 1854 to 1856. It was largely due to his efforts that the first railway in the highlands was born. *(J. Cook*

Above: The signal cabin at Dunrobin which was removed in 1902 and thereafter the signals and entrance to the Duke of Sutherland's carriage shed were controlled from a frame in the new station buildings. The signals at Dunrobin were taken out in 1906. *(Inverness Museum*

Below: A private station was provided at Dunrobin for the Duke and his two saloons were also kept there. The attractive station building seen here was done away with in favour of the present structure in 1902. *(Inverness Museum*

Top right: The second *Dunrobin* at Inverness with the magnificent saloon built in 1899 at Wolverton to the design of C. A. Park who, as the London and North Western Railway Carriage and Wagon Superintendent, used it as a prototype for the Royal Train of King Edward VII. The livery was a very dark green with gold lined white upper panels. The vehicle was used for overnight journeys and is fortunately preserved in the new railway museum at York. *(Inverness Museum*

Centre right: A 7 ton open wagon built for the Duke of Sutherland by the Gloucester Wagon Company in 1873. *(HMRS*

Bottom right: The day saloon, No 58A, which was built at Inverness in 1908 and also used in conjunction with the larger vehicle to steady the latter. This saloon along with *Dunrobin* is now in British Columbia. *(Courtesy Countess of Sutherland*

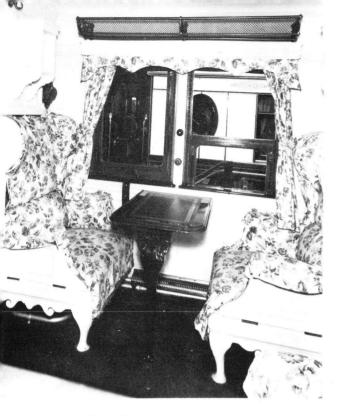

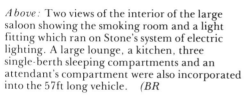

Above: Two views of the interior of the large saloon showing the smoking room and a light fitting which ran on Stone's system of electric lighting. A large lounge, a kitchen, three single-berth sleeping compartments and an attendant's compartment were also incorporated into the 57ft long vehicle.   *(BR*

Below: The station staff at Lairg c1910. Brown corduroy trousers were issued to most grades of station staff. The station master is John Campbell who was at Lairg from 1907 to 1914.
(R. M. Campbell

Above left: Frank McPhail, the last station master at Inverness before the grouping. He was appointed on 11th November, 1919 and retired on 31st November, 1931. *(Author's Collection*

Above right: Station Master John Campbell who was at Aviemore from c1900 to 1907 when he moved to Lairg. Only station masters at the more important stations had gold-braid hats. *(R. M. Campbell*

Below: First Aid practice in the goods yard at Inverness. In the background is brake van No 47 with what the Highland termed a 'dovecot window' although 'bird-cage' has become more usual terminology. *(J. Still*

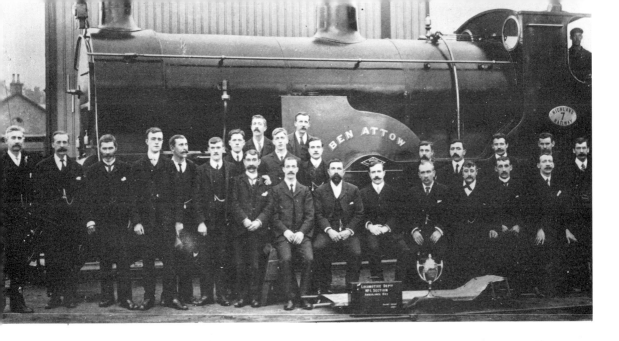

Top left: The Locomotive Department First Aid Team in front of one of Drummond's 'Small Bens'. The photograph was taken behind the Loco Signal Box adjacent to Lochgorm Works. Although the date and occasion are unknown, the No 1 section appear to have won the cup and the date would be between 1903 and 1912.   *(J. D. Watson*

Centre, bottom left: The worst accident which occurred on the Highland was on 18th June, 1914 when bridge No 237 collapsed following a cloudburst in the hills above Carr Bridge (LMS bridge number as the Highland named their bridges). The 11.50am from Perth to Inverness was derailed on the bridge over the Baddengorm Burn which had subsided slightly and soon after the train had come to a halt the bridge collapsed plunging one coach into the torrent and up-ending another two.   *(Author's Collection and A. F. Baird*

Below: The nature of this accident which occurred near Grantown is unknown. The note on the back of the photograph only records that the date was August 24th, 1914 and that the train was due to arrive at Grantown at 2.30am but was running two hours late. Most probably it was a case of runaway

wagons as anything of a more serious nature would have received wider publicity.   *(A. J. Bowie*

Top: An Inverness and Nairn Railway pass and a Morayshire Railway directors' ticket which at one time belonged to William Deuchar, passenger superintendent on the GNSR from 1900 to 1918, and are now in the possession of the GNSR Association.   *(Scottish Record Office*

Above: Works plate on $4-4-0$ tank No 17, formerly a $2-4-0$.   *(H. C. Casserley*

Left: A Highland handlamp manufactured by Hendry Brothers of Glasgow and used on the Aberfeldy branch. (A. J. Lambert

Far left: A carriage 'pot' lamp. Burning rape oil, these lamps were inserted through a hole which was generally covered by a metal cap during the day-time. (A. J. Lambert

Bottom left: The goods shed at Brora photographed in 1971. (A. J. Lambert

Above: The solebar plate off carriage No 1. (W. E. C. Watkinson

Right: The McKenzie and Holland finial predominated on the HR although Dutton, also of Worcester, supplied a number. The height is four feet. (A. J. Lambert

Below: Water tank and bag at Forsinard station. In Highland days a 'No water' board was attached to columns advising drivers where water supplies were temporarily unavailable. (A. G. Ellis

Above: The Culbin sands of Morayshire caused problems with sand drifting on the Burghead branch and the principle of the snow blower was applied to remedy the situation. The artificial trough is designed to deflect wind currents away from the line and so prevent blockage. The gentleman on the left is William Roberts, engineer-in-chief, and the photograph was taken in November 1900.   *(Author's Collection*

Below: A yard crane photographed at Halkirk station.   *(D. L. G. Hunter*

Above: With the grouping began a gradual transformation of the character of the Highland as standardisation and economy became the watchwords in the face of increasing road competition. In the field of motive power, standard LMS designs were to be seen on most of the main trains by the mid-thirties. The most common class was Stanier's Black Five and one of these is seen here with a southbound train at Golspie in BR days. On the right is the Duke of Sutherland's shed in which *Dunrobin* was kept. *(W. A. Camwell*

Below: The need for Great Western engines in the highlands was occasioned by the failure of the Dornoch branch engine in 1957. A suitable substitute was found in the pannier tank and two were sent to Helmsdale where Nos 1649 and 1646 are seen here on 21st June, 1960, a week after the complete closure of the Dornoch branch. One was kept as a spare engine at Helmsdale and the other at Dornoch. *(W. A. Camwell*

Acknowledgements

The list of acknowledgements is extensive and a testimony to the many and varied quarters from which much generous and willing help has come. To all the following I extend my grateful and sincere thanks:

Messrs J. G. Aird, J. H. L. Adams, V. R. Anderson, W. J. V. Anderson, Mrs A. F. Baird, Mr G. R. Barbour, Mrs P. Beal, Miss E. Barron, Messrs R. Berry, C. W. Black, A. J. Bowie, I. Brown, Miss M. Cameron, Messrs R. M. Campbell, H. C. Casserley, R. C. Chown, J. Cobban, J. Cook, the Countess of Sutherland, Messrs W. Davidson, G. A. Dixon, G. Dow, W. Dunnett, F. M. Dutton, A. G. Ellis, R. J. Essery, A. Gow, D. J. Grant, the Great North of Scotland Railway Association, Messrs A. M. Halley, E. W. Hannan, J. R. Hume, D. L. G. Hunter, the Historical Model Railway Society, Messrs K. Hoole, J. E. Kite, D. Johnstone, A. Kennedy, J. Kennedy, G. E. Langmuir, K. H. Leech, E. S. Lomax, Mrs M. Matheson, Mrs M. F. Matthew, Miss M. A. MacDonald, Messrs A. Macrae, J. McDonell, J. McIntosh, D. McKay, R. Milne, the Rev W.H. Nicholson, G. W. Osborne, H. G. N. Paterson, J. Pitman, B. Radford, M. Scott, Dr. I. Scrimgeour, G. Seaton, J. M. Sharman, Lt Col T. M. Simmons, C. R. Simpson, N. T. Sinclair, J. G. Spence, Mrs J. Still, Messrs S. S. Summers, W. R. Sutherland, J. M. Todd, La Vie du Rail, Messrs J. D. Watson, P. B. Whitehouse, E. Wilkinson, W. B. Yeadon, and J. Young.

The photographs by G. W. Wilson appear by courtesy of the Librarian of King's College Library, Aberdeen and those by K.A.C.R. Nunn by courtesy of the Locomotive Club of Great Britain. The photograph by W. H. C. Kelland appears by courtesy of the Bournemouth Railway Club.

In particular I must mention Messrs Ed McKenna and W. A. Camwell whose constant and ready help with advice and information has been invaluable: Finally Mr W. E. C. Watkinson for much kind assistance and the loan of the original painting for the frontispiece.